SPORTS ALL-ST★RS

SHOHEI OHTANI

Jon M. Fishman

Lerner Publications ◆ Minneapolis

SPORTS THRILLS
MEET
RESEARCH SKILLS

Lerner SPORTS

Free Database Trial: **lernersports.com**

Lerner Publications Company
An imprint of Lerner Publishing Group, Inc.
241 First Avenue North
Minneapolis, MN 55401 USA

For reading levels and more information, look up this title at www.lernerbooks.com.

Main body text set in Albany Std. Typeface provided by Agfa.

Editor: Lauren Foley
Lerner team: Sue Marquis

Library of Congress Cataloging-in-Publication Data

The Cataloging-in-Publication Data for *Shohei Ohtani* is on file at the Library of Congress.
ISBN 978-1-7284-6702-3 (lib. bdg.)
ISBN 978-1-7284-6703-0 (pbk.)
ISBN 978-1-7284-6704-7 (eb pdf)

Manufactured in the United States of America
1-51662-50401-10/14/2021

TABLE OF CONTENTS

Shohei Ohtani throws a pitch.

Shohei Ohtani was ready to throw. Standing on the pitcher's mound, he lifted his left leg. His knee rose to his chest. He stepped forward and threw the ball more than 90 miles (145 km) per hour. Strike!

- **Date of birth:** July 5, 1994

- **Position:** designated hitter (DH) and pitcher

- **League:** Major League Baseball (MLB)

- **Professional highlights:** started his pro baseball career in Japan; pitched and played DH in the 2021 MLB All-Star Game; had 46 home runs in 2021

- **Personal highlights:** grew up in Oshu, Japan; began playing baseball in second grade; lifted 495 pounds (225 kg) in an Instagram video

Ohtani begins to run around the bases after hitting a home run during a 2021 game against the Detroit Tigers.

Ohtani and the Los Angeles Angels faced off against the Detroit Tigers in August 2021. Ohtani's pitches zoomed across home plate. Some of them curved and sank. They were even harder to hit. Ohtani didn't allow a run until the fifth inning.

Ohtani is one of the best pitchers in MLB. He's also one of the league's most powerful hitters. In the eighth inning, he came up to bat with his team ahead 2–1.

The pitch flew over the middle of home plate. *Crack!* Ohtani swung and sent the ball soaring 430 feet (131 m) into the outfield seats.

The home run was Ohtani's 40th of the season. He also set an Angels record for most home runs in a season by a left-handed batter. Ohtani's blast gave the Angels a two-run lead, but he wasn't finished. He pitched the bottom of the eighth inning and retired three batters. The Angels won 3–1.

Ohtani's fans and teammates were amazed by his performance. Even Tigers manager A. J. Hinch was impressed. "Obviously, he's an incredibly special talent and we got to witness all of it firsthand tonight," Hinch said.

DOUBLE DUTY

Ohtani rounds the bases during a high school game.

Shohei Ohtani was born on July 5, 1994, in Oshu, Japan. He has an older brother, Ryuta, and an older sister, Yuka. Oshu lies in a rural area with many farms north of Tokyo.

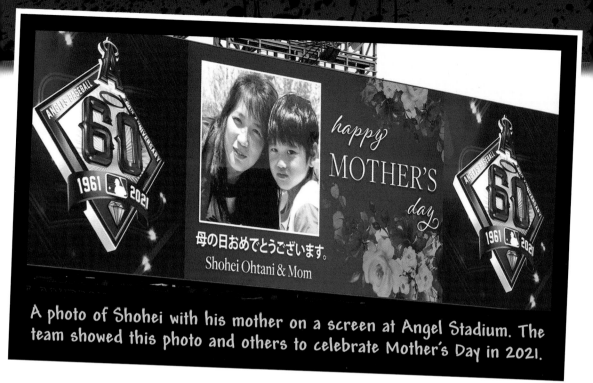

A photo of Shohei with his mother on a screen at Angel Stadium. The team showed this photo and others to celebrate Mother's Day in 2021.

In Japan, businesses often have sports teams that compete against teams from other companies. Players on these teams sometimes become pro athletes. Shohei's mother, Kayoko, played on a company badminton team. His father, Toru, played in the outfield on a baseball team for the same company.

Shohei was an active and fearless child. At the playground, he used equipment that had scared Ryuta at the same age. In his second year of elementary school, Shohei began playing baseball. His father became one of his coaches.

Ohtani winds up to throw a pitch during a game at Koshien Stadium in Japan in 2012.

From the beginning of his baseball career, Shohei was good at batting and pitching. As baseball players get older, they usually focus on one or the other. But Shohei was different. He wanted to do both. With practice, his pitches got faster and his batting improved.

Shohei played baseball at Hanamaki Higashi High School. In July 2012, he competed with his team in Summer Koshien, Japan's national high school baseball championship. In the sixth inning of a game, Shohei stood on the pitcher's mound. He zipped a pitch over home plate at 99 miles (160 km) per hour. Strike three! Shohei pumped his fist as the crowd cheered. His pitch was the fastest ever recorded in a high school game in Japan.

Fans couldn't wait to see Ohtani play in Nippon Professional Baseball (NPB), Japan's top league. But in October, he said he planned to join MLB instead. On October 25, NPB held its yearly draft. Despite Ohtani's desire to join MLB, NPB's Hokkaido Nippon-Ham Fighters chose him with the first overall pick.

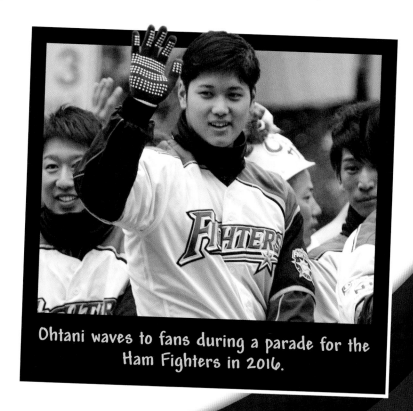

Ohtani waves to fans during a parade for the Ham Fighters in 2016.

The Ham Fighters convinced Ohtani to play for them. They told him it would be easier to start his pro career in Japan, close to his friends and family. They also promised to help him get ready for MLB and to let him go when he decided to leave.

Ohtani improved each season. In 2016, he led the Ham Fighters to the NPB championship. He became the first player to win the league's best pitcher and best DH awards in the same season. Ohtani was ready for MLB. The next year, he announced he was leaving Japan to play in the US.

Ohtani played for Japan's national team. In a 2016 game against the Netherlands, he hit a ball high and deep. The ball flew through the roof of the Tokyo Dome!

TWICE AS HARD

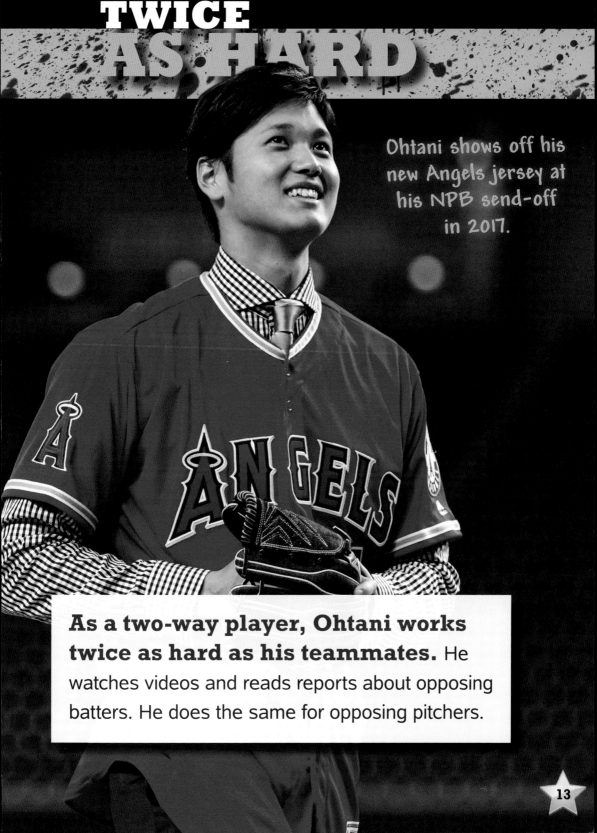

Ohtani shows off his new Angels jersey at his NPB send-off in 2017.

As a two-way player, Ohtani works twice as hard as his teammates. He watches videos and reads reports about opposing batters. He does the same for opposing pitchers.

Before games, Ohtani takes batting practice and warms up on the pitcher's mound. Other players focus on just batting or pitching.

Ohtani has devoted his life to his sport. "He eats, breathes, and sleeps baseball," said Anthony Bass, one of Ohtani's Ham Fighters teammates. In NPB, Ohtani played baseball, worked out, and improved his English language skills.

Ohtani throws a practice pitch before the 2021 MLB All-Star Game.

Ohtani warms up with his bat before every game.

Ohtani's hard work was evident to Micah Hoffpauir, another Ham Fighters teammate. "When [Ohtani] first got there, he was skinny," Hoffpauir said. "I mean really, really skinny." Ohtani was 6 feet 4 (1.9 m) and weighed 190 pounds (86 kg). He began lifting weights to get bigger and stronger. He soon weighed about 210 pounds (95 kg).

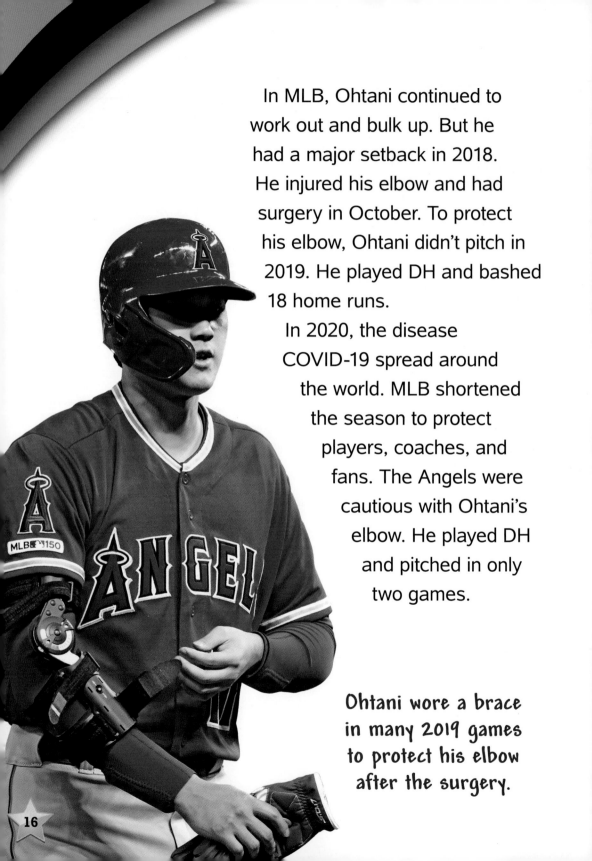

In MLB, Ohtani continued to work out and bulk up. But he had a major setback in 2018. He injured his elbow and had surgery in October. To protect his elbow, Ohtani didn't pitch in 2019. He played DH and bashed 18 home runs.

In 2020, the disease COVID-19 spread around the world. MLB shortened the season to protect players, coaches, and fans. The Angels were cautious with Ohtani's elbow. He played DH and pitched in only two games.

Ohtani wore a brace in many 2019 games to protect his elbow after the surgery.

After the season, Ohtani wanted to make sure his elbow was completely healthy for 2021. He took his workouts to a higher level. He packed on muscle and raised his weight to 225 pounds (102 kg).

Ohtani also made changes to his diet. He focused on eating healthful food that helped him perform better and recover from workouts more quickly. Ohtani's improved health and strength were evident in his bulging muscles. Angels fans couldn't wait to see him perform on the field.

In 2020, Ohtani showed off his strength on Instagram. He posted a video that showed him lifting 495 pounds (225 kg) from the floor to his hips.

Ohtani often signs photos, baseballs, and other objects for fans.

Angels fans often create signs to show their love for Ohtani.

Ohtani is one of the most popular athletes in the United States and Japan. His pitching and hitting skills are only part of his appeal. He's friendly with fans, answers questions from reporters, and never loses his easygoing manner. Fans also think he's handsome.

"He looks like a movie star," said baseball writer Robert Whiting.

Ohtani's popularity was revealed when fans voted for the 2021 MLB All-Star Game. He received 63 percent of the votes to play DH. MLB players and coaches later chose Ohtani to be the game's starting pitcher for the American League. He became the first player ever voted to play in the game as a pitcher and a hitter.

Ohtani throws a pitch during the first inning of the 2021 All-Star Game.

In April, Ohtani gave a signed bat to a charity auction. Money from the auction went to a project that helped buy masks and other gear for medical workers in Japan. "I'm sure it's hard for everyone," Ohtani said in Japanese. "But many people including the healthcare workers are working hard right now to solve this. I'm hoping that this will help them. I think we can support each other through this, with kindness, appreciation, and the thought of one another."

Ohtani helped provide medical workers in Japan with supplies like masks, glasses, and gloves.

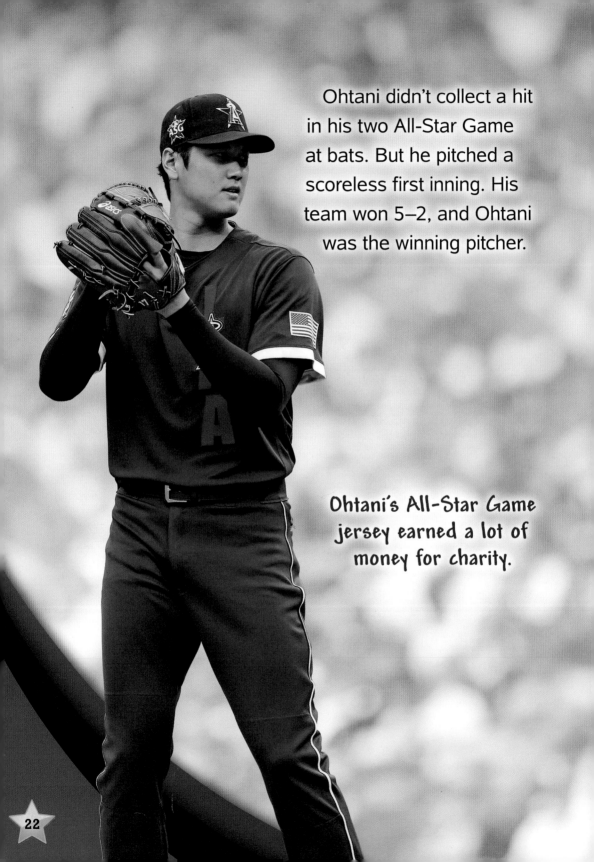

Ohtani didn't collect a hit in his two All-Star Game at bats. But he pitched a scoreless first inning. His team won 5–2, and Ohtani was the winning pitcher.

Ohtani's All-Star Game jersey earned a lot of money for charity.

Ohtani sprints toward first base during the All-Star Game.

After the All-Star Game, MLB auctioned the jersey Ohtani had worn. The auction closed at $130,210, setting an all-time record for MLB Auctions. The money went to the Baseball Assistance Team, a group that helps former baseball players, league employees, and their families. Ohtani had beaten his own record. A previous auction for an Ohtani game-worn jersey brought in $121,800. That money went to the Angels Baseball Foundation to help children with health care, education, and arts and sciences programs.

"ONCE IN A CENTURY"

Ohtani loves baseball and has fun on the field.

MLB played a full season in 2021. Ohtani was completely healed from his elbow injury. He put on a show that baseball fans had never seen before.

Ruth prepares to swing in 1925. He hit 714 career home runs, the most in MLB until Hank Aaron passed him in 1974.

Ohtani is often compared to MLB legend Babe Ruth. Ruth pitched and played in the outfield for the Boston Red Sox. In 1920, he joined the New York Yankees. Ruth was a good pitcher, but the Yankees rarely used him on the mound. They wanted him to focus on batting. Over the next 15 seasons, Ruth became MLB's greatest slugger. But he never played a complete season as a full-time hitter and pitcher.

In addition to hitting and pitching in the 2021 All-Star Game, Ohtani swung his bat in the Home Run Derby. He didn't win the event, but he still earned $150,000. He gave the money to people who work for the Angels.

In 2021, Ohtani pitched full-time for the Angels. On most days that he didn't pitch, he was the team's DH. He was one of the best players in the league at both positions.

Ohtani had a sparkling 9–2 record as a pitcher. He struck out 156 batters in 130 innings. He was even better with a bat in his hands. He finished third in the league in home runs with 46. He also finished in the top 10 in many other batting stats. Ohtani struck out more batters and hit more home runs in a single season than any MLB player before him.

Ohtani is unique in MLB. One sports official called him a "once in a century" player. And Ohtani is still in the prime of his career. Baseball fans will have many more chances to be amazed by his unhittable pitches and long home runs.

Ohtani focuses to aim his next pitch.

All-Star Stats

Ohtani is unique because he is one of the best pitchers and hitters on his team. Take a look at how he compared to his Angels teammates in home runs and strikeouts in 2021:

Home Runs by Angels Batters in 2021

1. Shohei Ohtani	46
2. Jared Walsh	29
3. Justin Upton	17
4. Max Stassi	13
5. Jack Mayfield	10

Strikeouts by Angels Pitchers in 2021

1. Shohei Ohtani	156
2. Andrew Heaney	113
3. Raisel Iglesias	103
4. Alex Cobb	98
5. Patrick Sandoval	94

Glossary

auction: a sale of property to the highest bidder

badminton: a game in which a shuttlecock is hit back and forth over a net by players using light rackets

blast: a home run

designated hitter (DH): a player who bats in place of the pitcher and who does not play a position in the field

draft: an event in which teams take turns choosing new players

manager: the head coach of a baseball team

pitcher's mound: the raised dirt area in the center of the infield from which the pitcher throws

pro: short for professional, taking part in an activity to make money

rural: relating to life in the country and farming

slugger: a hard-hitting batter

Source Notes

7 "Ohtani Dominates on Mound, Homers in 3–1 Angels Win," *ESPN*, August 18, 2021, https://www.espn.com/mlb /recap?gameId=401228857.

14 Ken Davidoff, "Shohei Ohtani's Desperation for Privacy Runs Deep," *New York Post*, December 5, 2017, https:// nypost.com/2017/12/05/the-levels-of-shohei-ohtanis -secrecy-run-deep/.

15 Ben Lindbergh, "Inside Shohei Ohtani's Superhero Origin Story," Ringer, July 12, 2021, https://www.theringer.com /mlb/2021/7/12/22573272/shohei-ohtani-first-two-way -season-nippon-ham-fighters.

20 Doug Miller, "Fans Taken by Ohtani's Set of Skills, Innocence," MLB, November 29, 2017, https://www.mlb .com/news/a-look-at-the-history-of-shohei-ohtani -c262589034.

21 Scott Polacek, "Angels Issue $1.2M in Payments to Stadium Employees amid Coronavirus Hiatus," *Bleacher Report*, April 19, 2020, https://bleacherreport.com/articles /2887494.

27 Jabari Young, "MLB Has Big Plans for Shohei Ohtani, a 'Once in a Century' Player," CNBC, July 13, 2021, https:// www.cnbc.com/2021/07/13/shohei-ohtani-a-once-in-a -century-player-and-mlb-has-big-plans-for-him.html.

Fishman, Jon M. *Baseball's G.O.A.T.: Babe Ruth, Mike Trout, and More*. Minneapolis: Lerner Publications, 2020.

Kortemeier, Todd. *Shohei Ohtani: Baseball Star*. Lake Elmo, MN: Focus Readers, 2019.

Levit, Joe. *Babe Ruth: Super Slugger*. Minneapolis: Lerner Publications, 2021.

Official Los Angeles Angels Website
https://www.mlb.com/angels

Shohei Ohtani Stats, Fantasy & News
https://www.mlb.com/player/shohei-ohtani-660271

T-Mobile Home Run Derby
https://www.mlb.com/all-star/home-run-derby

Index

Photo Acknowledgments

Image credits: Mark Cunningham/MLB Photos/Getty Images, pp. 4–5; Gregory
Shamus/Getty Images, p. 6; Kyodo News/Contributor/Getty Images, pp. 8–11;
Masterpress/Contributor/Getty Images, p. 13; Rob Tringali/Stringer/Getty Images,
pp. 14–15; AP Photo/Nick Wosika/Icon Sportswire, p. 16; Stephen Maturen/Stringer/
Getty Images, p. 18; Harry How/Getty Images, p. 19; Adam Glanzman/Stringer/Getty
Images, p. 20; Natale Zanardi/Shutterstock.com, p. 21; Mary DeCicco/Stringer/Getty
Images, p. 22; Daniel Shirey/Stringer/Getty Images, p. 23; Dustin Bradford/Stringer/
Getty Images, p. 24; The Stanley Weston Archive/Contributor/Getty Images, p. 25;
Jayne Kamin-Oncea/Contributor/Getty Images, p. 27.

Cover: Tony Gutierrez/AP/Shutterstock.com; John McCoy/AP/Shutterstock.com.